King Lear of the Taxi

Musings of a New York City Actor/Taxi Driver

Davidson Garrett

Advent Purple Press

New York

King Lear of the Taxi
Musings of a New York City Actor/Taxi Driver

Copyright © April 2006 by Davidson Garrett

ISBN-10: 0-9774446-0-0
ISBN-13: 978-0-9774446-0-1

Library of Congress Control Number 2005909680

First Printing
Printed and bound in Canada by Art Bookbindery
www.artbookbindery.com

Cover Design by Yvonne Parks, Art Bookbindery

For Roger Anderson

Acknowledgements

The following poems originally appeared in these publications:

"Taxi Driver" *The New York Times* © 1999 by The New York Times Co. Reprinted by Permission

"Coffee Break" originally titled "Contemplating Caviar" *The Unknown Writer Poetry Supplement 2002*

"Blasted Out of Dixie" *Sensations Magazine Issue 32/ Winter 2003*

"A Taxi Driver's Die Götterdämmerung" *Sensations Magazine Issue 33/Spring 2004*

"Spring Forth" *Sensations Magazine Issue 38/Spring 2005*

This book evolved from a chapbook manuscript entitled *Taxi Dreams* which was a finalist in the Gival Press Chapbook Competition in 2000. I would like to thank Dean Kostos, Darielle Rayner, Rita Montana, Jessica Nooney, and Nina Klippel for their helpful feedback in the early development.

For the current book, I would like to thank Velma Jean Reeb, John J. Trause, Rita Montana, Roger Anderson, Lissette Gutiérrez, and The Wild Angels Poets and Writers Group at the Cathedral of St. John the Divine for their suggestions and loving support.

I would like to thank Joseph Wisniewski, William Traylor, William Toner, Roger Anderson, and Clyde Wachsberger for their friendship and humor that helped get me through this project.

A special thanks to Enid Nemy of *The New York Times* for publishing "Taxi Driver," in The Metropolitan Diary, which gave me the idea for this book, and to David Messineo, publisher of *Sensations Magazine,* for his inspiration and encouragement.

You are enough. Don't act, just be: simple words of wisdom from my first acting teacher at the American Academy of Dramatic Arts. Simple, yet profound and confusing to a nimble twenty-year-old just off the plane from Louisiana, beginning a new life in the exciting—but terrifying—city of New York. Discovering myself through the dramas of Miller, Inge, and, of course, Shakespeare, was an electrifying awakening and a triumphant failure. Being myself was not an easy concept to grasp. I had much more fun just enunciating lines and hamming up dramatic scenes to get as many laughs as possible. Needless to say, my unrefined gifts were not appreciated by the instructors nor by the fellow thespians-in-training.

It was only a couple of summers later that I experienced a real awakening. I ventured to Stratford, Connecticut for a production of *King Lear* at the renowned American Shakespeare Festival—starring the magnificent classical actor Morris Carnovsky. His riveting portrayal reflected the grand sweep of Shakespeare's language, but more importantly, the subtlety and intimacy of a man's life in total ruins. Carnovsky's historic interpretation made me weep, and it enhanced my understanding of the power of versified words spoken from the deepest chambers of the heart. After the play had ended, I strolled out of the legendary theater into a late afternoon thunderstorm, a changed being, filled with a renewed hope and a yearning to perfect my craft as an actor, perhaps someday to have the privilege of attempting King Lear, and hopefully, to achieve the introspection and artistic nuance of the performance I had just witnessed. This was a daunting goal, but a spiritual rebirth to drive me onward in the never-ending pursuit of my own inward truth.

Unfortunately, most actors in the United States rarely have the opportunity of playing King Lear. Acting in America is usually a commercial endeavor—and actors often need to accept roles in soap operas or feature films in order to be able to perform plays in low-paying regional theaters or Off-Off Broadway. As we pursue our calling, we must find survival work to keep us afloat in a city notorious for an inflation rate that multiplies by the week.

For over twenty-five years, my survival job has been driving a taxi. The cab has given me the required flexibility to attend auditions, to take unpredictable time off for occasional work in film or television, and more significantly, to study humanity from my rearview mirror.

Many of the poems and prose pieces in this book were born in the taxi—parked in front of nightclubs in the wee hours of the morning while waiting for fares. A few lines were scribbled on meter receipt tape at red lights in heavy traffic. I also wrote during grueling hours working as a stand-in on independent films, where, between takes on the set, I would hastily sketch story ideas in notebooks.

I have not performed King Lear as of this writing. However, an actor always needs something to anticipate, a challenge to march toward. The hard-to-reach heaven keeps us pliant. It is also character-building, we're told.

Davidson Garrett
December 2005

Table of Contents

I have full cause of weeping, but this heart
shall break into a hundred thousand flaws,
or ere I'll weep.—O, Fool, I shall go mad!

King Lear   Act 2 Scene 4

Spring Forth

A neurotic nimbus cloud
    swirls in a mercurial sky,
thunders a scream viciously loud,

quickly, under our house I fly.
    The flimsy frame upon stone blocks
hovers inches overhead, my

calves scrape against sharp rocks
    silently resting from ancient days,
long before time was marked by clocks.

Through screened siding pupils gaze
    at rain tumbling in pinched light—
painting the yard an olive haze,

electrified day sizzles into night.
    Adult footsteps above eerily creak
as lizards crawl at close-range sight,

voices inside the wooden home shriek
    "life is hell and we are damned afraid"—
cracked floorboards let madness leak.

The furious wind advances its raid
    releasing a flood of pent-up fears—
bursting like worn dams—decayed,

spouting from my eyes torrential tears.
    Yearning to be rid of constant moping,
kitchen-sink vision that never clears,

this dark hiding place is fine for coping
    from weathered souls bereft of art—
who kill pastel hopes with deadly roping.

Secret plans harbor in my child's heart.
    I lie on damp earth and plot escape
—someday a pink caveman will depart.

Beneath the foundation becomes a cape
    covering snugly from water and lightning
while manic gods assault the land by rape.

Under the house dreams are tightening
    as the tempest becomes less frightening.

At Sixteen

O precious wheels, my way out today,
    driving madly a getaway course—
        I burn rubber on a bayou freeway,

primal scream until quite hoarse—
    "I'm free world—what do'ya think?"
        Peeping up to the egg-yoke source

fat-boy sun fires forth a naughty wink,
    I twang country-western songs off-key,
        high on sugar & vitamins with zinc.

Airborne, no other autos whiz by me,
    flying fast like on Indianapolis' track—
        a pimpled teenager no longer to be.

Never-ever caught & dragged back,
    waking up in NYC, seeing stars—
        living on movie magazines & a Big Mac.

Soon realizing laws forbid stealing cars,
    even to escape mother's fawning pate—
        back to home, might as well be Mars.

My proper parents would seal my fate
    if I wrecked their Ford, returned home late.

Blasted Out of Dixie

My final farewell conjures darkness,
passionate teardrops of freezing rain
fall from a sky sobbing golf-ball hail
surprising the slumbering New South,
blanketing weary magnolias with snow,
turning its fertile land into thick ice.

An eight-hundred-mile drive on ice
ahead, my car flees in winter darkness
a town buried under glacial snowdrifts—
more accustomed to gentle spring rain
and lyrical breezes singing southerly,
than for precision bombing by hard hail.

The perilous odyssey brings *Hail
Marys* to the lips—as the blue auto ice
capades on the slippery highway, south
of the river that evokes gothic darkness—
while the white night vies for a regal reign,
battling the moonlight with clouded snow.

Vicksburg surrenders to the Snow
Queen, lazy tongues declare—*hail
has frozen over*, raging gods rain
wrath with sharp arrows of dry ice
to punish prejudice toward skin of darkness
in this frigid heart of the Bible-belt South.

Recollections of a boyhood in the South
flood a tired mind, recalling snow
jobs by cross-burning fools of darkness
wearing hooded choir robes—hailing
Satan as they packed black bodies on ice—
washing the blood away with dirty rain.

On the road a last time, nostalgia rains
on the brain, in this timeless, surreal, South.
Suddenly, a service station stop for iced
Coke, to numb my body cold as snow—
never to forget the cold trajectory—of the hail
of *KILL HOMOS*—blasting me out of darkness.

Rain, snow, hail, ice,
a tempest only befits my Southern goodbye—
as I escape the darkness of hate.

Welcome to New York

Ya'think you're so unique, Buster?
Get a grip on your ass!
There's a million others just like'ya
All clawing for the same prize.

Get a grip on your ass!
Busloads of dreamers arrive daily,
All clawing for the same prize.
You're a competitive cliché, Sweetheart.

Busloads of dreamers arrive daily!
Take a look in the mirror Handsome.
You're a competitive cliché, Sweetheart,
Just another noodle in the pot.

Take a look in the mirror Handsome.
Ya'blend in with the other losers,
Just another noodle in the pot.
Wake up and smell the Chock Full O' Nuts!

Ya'blend in with the other losers,
Burn'ya Doris Day flicks.
Wake up and smell the Chock Full O' Nuts,
Go out and buy some bulldozer balls!

Burn'ya Doris Day flicks.
Don't quit your day-job Honey-Lamb,
Go out and buy some bulldozer balls!
Ya'think you're so unique, Buster?

Dramatic Arts

At the academy, massive sledge hammers
beat egos to fine pulp. We must forget
theorized, university-driven dogma
formerly drummed into our heads

in the hinterlands of Arkansas or Alabama.
Acting, a hallowed vocation, fully deserves
the same reverence as a deity. Boleslavsky
and Stanislavsky become new role models.

Voice and diction, Russian ballet, make-up,
scene-study, fencing; a traditional classic
curriculum to fine-tune body-instruments,
a multi-disciplined approach for longevity

in the theater, or if we are desperate—film.
Through the halls, glossy photos line the walls
of dazzling alumni. Grace Kelly and Robert Redford
glitter alongside Jason Robards and Thelma Ritter.

Twenty-year-olds, dentalize Will Shakespeare
and Euripides, filled with fame-lust, drooling at
glamorous 8x10 headshots, visualizing our own flashy
Broadway débuts, complete with lavish dressing rooms,

laminated stars of gold on jet-black doors.
In a short time, the celebrated instructors—
mostly unemployed actors, weed out the pretty
from the ugly. We learn the harsh truth

about show business. Natural beauty
will gain access to scouts of talent
swifter than sensitive arm-waving trolls
reciting Hamlet's pensive soliloquies.

Lessons of advice abound from bitter-hearted teachers, their graying lives tragically wasted by years of rejections. Our major revelation gleaned through high-toned double talk:

Find cheap rent and easy day-jobs!

Taxi Driver

Yellow zephyr in the dark night
speeds onward to subsidize
the worker's meager existence—
imprisons a scorched spirit
and reduces earned hopefulness
to a short break for spaghetti
as he dines in still solitude
at a greasy-spoon dive—
soon to be locked behind the wheel
for hours, while the brain plays games
with bold dreams that disappear
when the red light blinks back to green.

Movie Extra in Central Park

Eager as an anxious child,
longing for discovery on the outdoor set—
I pray my crowd scene

will ignite my cinematic career
and explode me to stardom
as in the bygone glitz

of old Hollywood. Fat chance
of such sweet serendipity:
that dance with destiny

happens only to babes in sweaters
sipping sodas at drugstore fountains.
Undaunted, like a thoroughbred thespian,

I breathe redolent air
inside the emerald oasis
musing happily for the moment—

soon to give a pure offering of my art,
captured eternally by sacred celluloid
in the spilt second of an eye's blink.

Graveyard Shift in the Taxi Garage Waiting Room

Peppermint brew gulped down the throat
soothes my saturnine soul

soon to embark on a five-borough odyssey
ending with the first peek of morning sun.

As night slumbers, distant cars sputter
like snoring wind; under bright fluorescents

I ponder where on this whirling planet
my upside-down heart hides?

Is it beneath the urine-soaked oak
that embellishes the stone sidewalk

across from the body shop—
or atop an alabaster skyscraper

ready for a fatal jump? Did it die
years ago from thieving cavaliers

who tossed it cruelly
to hungry dogs for meat?

Wherever rapturous love has gone
it is far from this lonesome purgatory

where I wait to be dispatched—
wondering if my first fare will be heaven or hell.

On the Couch

For Sheldon Firstenberg

Year after year,
the Freudian doctor
cautiously guides me
through early childhood
and a bullied adolescence,
a weekly excavation of my inner self,
digging deeply to examine lifelong trauma—
understanding at last why I embraced drama.

A Brush with Holiness

Several years ago, Mother Teresa of Calcutta was in New York staying at one of her mission houses in the South Bronx. I had first heard about her on *The Mike Douglas Show*. She picked up dying children in her arms and saved them like an ambulance of mercy, unafraid of snotty noses or body stench. Impressive! In those days I wanted to be a saint too.

daily rejections by gatekeepers of art
    haunt me
striving for a golden needle in a burned-out haystack
    my mind's fuzzy focus becomes maroon clouds
    of self-doubt
discouragement fuels an inward search
    through religion
weekly novenas for a numbed-out actor
    verging on breakdown

I tried to attend Mass everyday, High Church Episcopal, of course. On Sundays I was an acolyte at the most holy altar of God. Many weekend nights I spent praying in a fancy retreat house with old-fashioned Anglican sisters who wore traditional habits. Monastic discipline: a perfect sedative for lifelong guilt-addiction.

in dreams my mother's voice wails
    "get up you good-for-nothing teenager—
Sunday morning is for Church and saying Amen—
    hell is for those who miss choir practice
to watch The Wizard of Oz*"*

On a spur-of-the-moment lark one Saturday evening, while driving my leased cab in Manhattan, I pulled over to a coin payphone and called Mother Teresa's convent in Mott Haven, asked the puzzled voice who answered if

I could come immediately and meet the great lady from the continent of curry. The snappy sister said tersely, "No, Mother Teresa is resting."

snubbed by nuns,
*   don't they know who I am—(I wish I did)*
I've absorbed the writings of Thomas Merton
*   and Dorothy Day—*
worked as a stand-in for Woody Allen movies
*   burned the television screen with pizzazz*
on All My Children

I had recently read in the newspaper that M.T. was returning to her slummy streets of Calcutta early the next morning, I presumed after the Eucharist. I started saying The Rosary in my yellow jail, praying devoutly for my big chance to rub elbows with a flesh and blood saint!

Hail Mary full of grace,
*   help this hopeless Queen*
find destiny's rightful place

In a pensive mood, I debated whether I should just scoot up to the Bronx and park quietly like a private eye—and wait near Mother Teresa's building, perhaps to get a tiny glimpse of pure heaven from a distance— before the departure for India. After all, even in celebrity-filled New York, it's rare to spot a really big- time, religious legend.

actor/ taxi driver
*   economically chained behind the wheel*
always seeking spiritual direction
*   passengers don't believe I'm an aspiring artist*
think I'm a smooth-talking horserace gambler

After a tedious night chauffeuring club kids, I sped to a desolate area of the South Bronx, sat patiently inside the taxi across from the residence of the wrinkled nun, and watched for the sun to rise on what was to be an electric day.

neighborhood of bombed-out buildings
background setting for a Scorsese film—
air redolent with dogshit
eerie howls of cat-hookers—
hell sleeps not-so-soundly
under the shrouded sky of Mott Haven

Word of the imminent departure had spread, and a crowd of religious groupies gathered before the convent entrance—as the sky turned crimson streaking into a bright dawn. There was great excitement knowing any moment the humble recipient of the Nobel Peace Prize would stroll out of her dwelling, buckle-up inside a rusted van—and be whisked quickly away to JFK. At last, I would finally get my once-in-a-lifetime opportunity to witness holiness incarnate. Ecstatic fervor engulfed me!

all my life waiting to see God
in a tangible circle of light—
waiting for the peace that passes
all understanding—
waiting for a glance at eyes
of iron-gripping faith

After a while the door opened, and nuns in blue and white saris streamed out onto the sidewalk—processing in front of the glowing woman of God. Many jubilant well-wishers greeted the divine one and she returned their affection with smiles and hugs. When Mother Teresa passed by me, I knelt down and tried to kiss her hand. She said, "Please don't do that" and waved her arms in playful disgust as she brushed me aside and moved on through the screams of the faithful.

shell-shocked back to reality
by the indifferent blood of a breathing icon—
brushed off like lint on a sari
swept aside like loose trash cluttering the sidewalk

I drove back downtown somewhat dejected. Soon I would tell my parish priest how I'd almost kissed the spiritual star's hand. Although it was now Pentecost Sunday, a bit of fire had been zapped from my breast. The miffed Father was unimpressed. He chastised me because I was late for Mass and had failed to light the altar candles on time. This was the same priest who sometimes cursed in the sacristy.

"its a privilege and duty to serve at God's table
don't ever forget it—gentlemen of the altar"

God works in mysterious ways. Leaving that Episcopal church that spring morning, feeling the hollowness of the previous experiences, my innocent eyes were opened as I realized even saints and religious institutions have their earthly maculations—amid love and good works. I also knew my days of swinging incense and lighting altar candles would soon cease, as my rocky road to spiritual enlightenment began to take a different route.

on a new journey with improved maps
and more comfortable shoes—
great saints live among us in our everyday lives
not only in convents and ornamented cathedrals
my revised philosophy:
forgive, love, continue the journey, have sex and eat—
a real epiphany

Inside the Gates of Economic Prison

Inmates rarely relish the taste of sweet bail
When given a long sentence in Poverty Jail.

A daily dungeon fortified with invisible walls—
Steadfastly strengthened when credit-rating falls.

Menial labor guarantees to make vertebrae ache,
While dining is on ground horse instead of steak.

Prison uniforms, forget designer jeans from Saks,
Instead they're rags, drooping from thrift-store racks.

Cheap recreation will be provided by network TV,
Never fascinating cable, that costs money you see.

Monotony flies by writing poems through the night,
On brown paper bags because of pocketbook blight.

Loan sharks swim near, but seldom are they nice—
Unfortunately, it's difficult to file bankruptcy twice.

Bopping around town is quite a problem to meet,
One solution: nurse angry blisters on worn-out feet.

Home Sweet Home isn't warbled in high-rise luxury,
It's whistled in a tenement, where society rats take tea.

Never plan exotic trips to Zanzibar or Thailand,
Poor folks are fortunate if they ferry to Staten Island.

There are few paid artists in this imprisoned state—
Creative spirits alongside stock brokers hardly rate.

This torturous life boring, the rich don't give a tear,
To them, insignificant paupers should quietly disappear.

Severe illness becomes a blueprint for a burial tomb,
Without insurance, one croaks in the Emergency Room.

The iron gates of escape lock tightly all too well,
When doing time *in the slammer* of financial hell.

My Day at Bellevue
or Without Health Insurance in America

You heavens give me that patience, patience I need.
King Lear Act 2, Scene 4

In labyrinthine halls mobbed with humanity, my nostrils get a whiff of institutional perfume, astringent Ajax. Bright fluorescents illuminate black signs with arrows: Out Patient Clinic, Emergency, Pediatrics, Pharmacy. My tingling back pain swiftly urges me to Emergency.

A snarl-faced policeman instructs me to stand in line for an interrogation by a triage nurse. Through plexi-glass, two Mexican brothers furiously squawk, an open steel door allows their broken-English to escape—as one interprets to a confused Florence Nightingale in a pea-green uniform. She scribbles answers to standard hospital questions from the olive-skin immigrants, an ailing sibling places hand over heart and mimes anguish. The medic writes and writes and writes—stopping her chicken-scratch to take the required temperature and pulse. Finally, the brooding, checked-out duo, are ordered to a holding area.

I hobble into a cramped office decorated with rusty furniture. My social security number is given along with vital statistics. Nurse Frantic asks bluntly, "Do you have health insurance?"

"No I don't have health insurance," I grimly answer.

The sister of mercy stares deeply into my sky-blue eyes and trumpets like an angry drill sergeant, "Why are you here?"

"A mysterious rash causing pricking needles in my back," I mutter painfully to play on her sympathy.

Oodles of more paperwork, tongue-throat check, heart analysis, more paperwork and a dismissive shout: "Get thee to the waiting room!"

Two hours of bench-sitting later, an overworked aide beckons me through doors leading to a curtained cubicle stuffed with a cot-like stretcher and medical tools.

After some time, a short Pakistani physician appears; he demands a urine sample in a plastic cup. I squirt only three drops of yellow juice from behind a paper screen, emerging in a washed-out hospital gown, my sleepwear for a long nap on the examining plank.

The little doctor returns and huffs, "What's your problem?" He spots crimson blotches and wonders if it could be mild eczema caused by overly-harsh laundry detergent?

Enter Stage Left, an Asian female in a starched white coat. Her weary eyes squint at inflamed dots on cream-colored skin. On cue, with a surly snap—"Give him hydro-cortisone cream!"

The two tired Residents exit Stage Right.

I continue my dozing imagining imminent death. Islamabad's pride and joy soon awakens me and declares: "Urine OK, take pain killers for complaining back, visit a dermatologist in our out-patient clinic. Unfortunately, the next available appointment is one month from now."

I grumble, "What if I die before that time?"

Dr. Too Busy whines, "You probably won't, but if you think you are—rush back to the Emergency Room."

My divine revelation: I've discovered Bellevue's little scheme. This is how they drive people CRAZY to fill their psychiatric wards!

Stranded on the Brooklyn Queens Expressway

Blow, winds, and crack your cheeks! Rage, blow!
King Lear Act 3, Scene 2

Cables in my hand, please don't drive by,
My taxi's battery has decided to die—
The weather is frigid, my blue fingers cold,
I need the good Samaritan from days of old.

Cables in my hand, all I need is a quick charge,
Your time will be short, my appreciation large.
I stand on this highway freezing in fear—
Surely I'll perish before any help is near.

Cables in my hand, a Chevy and a Ford
Both pass me by—I'm snubbed and ignored.
No sympathy at all for my dramatic plight,
Only urban indifference on this black night.

Cables in my hand, a truck splashes muck,
—I'm certainly experiencing cabdriver luck.
Turning tables would I assist another man—
If he were holding jumper cables in his hand?

Twelve Winters Living at the YMCA

A coziness invades this hole-in-the-wall room,
the frigid earth is blanketed with soft white stillness

as tiny amounts of steam perk through a rusty radiator—
a cacophonous piping gives the day its winter beat.

Patches of cracked ceiling decorate the abode,
peeling green plaster and Aunt Mattie's quilt

jazz-up the joint with crazy color
while thoughts of art, music, and literature

abound in the reflections of the dweller. No kitchen
and a shared toilet keep the ego humble,

a clutter of all worldly possessions sprinkle the room
with atmosphere. Questions infiltrate my monk's cell.

Is this a quality lifestyle for a technological century?
How does the world view my meager existence

in the realm of progress? Each philosophical idea
is given due consideration, often with uneasiness.

And then mystically, like Advent light, a remembrance
of an artistic calling—comforts my quixotic mind.

The ingredients for the maintenance of a rhapsodic spirit
are hidden in all the dog-eared books and faded keepsakes.

As the snowflakes fly, an inner warmth of hope
still kindles the fire of future expectations. For today,

the room is safe, toasty, and without pretensions.
It is home.

Coffee Break

A corpulent couple
seated next to me at a coffee bar
contemplates a newly purchased jar

of caviar. They study the glass container
earnestly, resembling Nobel-prize-winning scientists
gazing upon micro-organisms. Each printed

word on the label is read aloud:
name of product; export city; port of entry;
ingredients; net weight;—price.

The precious morsels are held in triumph—
as if ravenous refugees had found
the last scrap of food on earth

after the devastation of war. Around and around
the man and woman turn the hallowed fish eggs,
their excited tongues full of salivary

sensuousness. Soon they depart
and I wonder if the epicurean delicacy
will ever be consumed—

or will it become a secret idol of worship
upon which a jeweled tabernacle is built
to house it in their kitchen?

Coloratura Cabby

A summer shower tickles the taxi windshield,
I speed like an automaton to Kennedy Airport—
a Maurice Chevalier-type behind my head
munches potato chips. After swiftly delivering

this French cargo to Departures, I glumly discover
deserted Arrivals, forcing me to turnaround back
to the Daedalian city, my back seat empty. Distressed
by pockets of poverty,

I play Vincenzo Bellini's tragic opera
Beatrice di Tenda—on my cheap—but treasured
cassette player. Miss Joan Sutherland
laments the inequitable world

with limpid bel canto supplications. Diesel-fumed air
pummels my face unmercifully—
I rocket fearlessly on the Grand Central Parkway
immolating tires, the coloratura virtuosity

keeps the motorcar musically airborne.
My former passenger off to Parisian leisure
and I am confined to workaday—inCARceration.
Like forlorn sopranos, taxi drivers

have mad scene cabalettas too;
our orchestral accompaniments—
honking horns by out-of-tempo Jersey drivers
instead of well-paid union musicians

maneuvering perfectly pitched scales—
documented eternally. A grand opera
may have its final dénouement, but a hack's life
grinds out long unending acts.

Day after day—night after night,
the public clamors for us with raised arms.
As we slave behind the wheel, only off-duty lights
send audiences away after frenzied standing ovations.

The Backscratcher

Varnished stick, paralyzed hand,
curved fingers delighting

impossible-to-reach flesh
without aid of polished nails.

Made by exploited Chinese workers,
sold by underpaid immigrants

to tourists perusing cheap stalls
on Mott Street. Faithful friend, you gloriously relieve

a never-ending, irritating itch
from shoulder blades soaked by beads of sweat,

souvenirs of my back-breaking job—
comforted by your pleasurable palm.

Bacall in my Back Seat

Peering through the taxi's rearview mirror, I saw Lauren Bacall in my back seat. The actress had hailed the yellow chariot with one gloved palm in front of Mortimers, asking to be transported to The Dakota. Strange, I would have presumed the movie star traveled in her own black limousine with an English chauffeur named Cedric.

At first I didn't recognize her through the translucence of the cab's partition window. Seated behind my bald crown next to the left rear door, the bright streetlights of Lexington Avenue resplendently illuminated her high cheekbones—but it was Lauren's Chaliapin-like voice—requesting I take the 66th Street transverse—that confirmed her regal presence.

Prior to her swirling unexpectedly into my world of the kitchen-sink drama—*The Woeful Taxi Driver*—the evening had flourished with supreme boredom as my pecuniary state had reached rock bottom. To placate the ennui of the torturous job, I had eaten a junk-food dinner, heavy with imitation lard—making my stomach feel especially bloated as it protruded over dirty blue jeans, tightening an over-burdened belt buckle. Despite my caffeine-drenched brain, a second wind revived my rotten mood to attend to this unanticipated advent of Hollywood Royalty.

Ordinarily, it is not my practice to initiate trivial banter with passengers, but it had been many moons since I'd had a recent Oscar nominee sitting at arm's length gazing at the back of my glimmering egghead.

"Congratulations on your latest Oscar nomination Miss Bacall!" A polite thank you was murmured and she continued to sit with insouciance, like a freshly poured dry martini.

Lucky for her, my mother had trained me with proper etiquette and I didn't become an obsequious bug-eyed groupie who just got off the boat from the land of the hicks.

Should I interrupt the hushed silence with idle small-talk I pondered? After all, I had proudly worked as an extra on the celebrity's picture, *The Mirror Has Two Faces*, and we had both been directed by BARBRA STREISAND!

I rationalized that Miss Betty and I were both working thespians—though her acting fees were significantly higher than mine. Since Fate had tossed us momentarily together in the same automobile, this not-exactly-Einstein deduction of mine—quickly made the awkwardness vanish.

As I drove the clamorous vehicle through Central Park with cool spring air blustering through opened windows, the queen of quintessential New York Class—Miss Bacall that is—loosened up and commented on the unpredictable weather.

Using her chit-chat as an ice breaker, I assumed she was beginning to take a trifling interest in my humble situation, perhaps—Discover Me!

Flattery began to pour like honey from my adoring lips as I lied gingerly, pretending to have seen all her movies at least twice, until she graciously reminded me that I recalled one with Bette Davis and not her. Behind the taxi's greasy steering wheel, I became an instant expert on her legendary career in show-biz. Babbling on, I navigated with utmost care to deliver this rare treasure safely. God forbid I should have a wreck and break her famous face!

My zestful apotheosis made her eyes glow as I continued my encomium for her contributions to mankind and the universe. Finally, arriving in front of her fortress of an apartment building, the celluloid luminary paid me the meter's price through the cage window—along with a handsome tip.

I proclaimed she should perform the leading role in Tennessee Williams' *Sweet Bird of Youth*.

"I did that in London" she answered, while fiddling to open the door in the murky light. Gracefully, Mrs. Bogart emerged onto the sidewalk of West 72nd Street—and I watched her as she strode like a monarch through the massive iron gates where John Lennon had been assassinated.

Silently, with a bittersweet smile, I motored away into the dark canyons of film noir skyscrapers, musing about the serendipitous moments in a hack's life—while searching for my next fare.

Prominent Persons In My Cab
or They Had Their Lives In My Hands

...preeminence, and all the large effects
that troop with majesty
King Lear Act 1, Scene 1

Martha Graham John Kander Fred Ebb Arlene Francis (twice) Anna Kisselgoff Frank Rich Hermine Gingold Kristine Chenoweth Joshua & Nedda Harrington Logan Eileen Myles Sylvia Miles Rocco Landesman Leslie Uggams Julie Halston Marge Redmond Charlie Rose Ron Kuby Gene Shalit Celeste Holm Parker Posey (twice) Tim Robbins Susan Sarandon George C. Wolf Regina Resnick Ewa Poodles Katherine Hellman Marilyn Hacker Rachel Hadas Alice Quinn Bella Abzug Alfred Urey Issac Stern Lauren Bacall Aprile Millo Joel Grey Cicely Tyson Kevin Kline Risë Stevens Georgia Engels Dolora Zajick Phillip Semour Hoffman Ron Silver Ben Vereen's mother Christo & Jeanne-Claude Kathy Lee Gifford Carole Shelly Robert Knight Michael Knight Iris Love Liz Smith Bill Boggs Tammy Grimes Sarah Billinghurst Mrs. George London James King John Alexander Dame Edna a k a Barry Humphries Simon Winchester Richard Bernstein Joe Franklin Madeline Kahn (twice) Judy Collins (twice) Leslie Stahl Nicky Silver Pia Lindstrom Joseph Stein Dr. Joy Brown Stephen Weber Edmund White Judy Gold Robert McNeil Charlayne Hunter-Gault Moises Kaufman Paul Jacobs Stanley Drucker Blance Wissen Cook Angus McIndoe Dominick Dunne Gail Robinson David Rothenberg Pat Collins Hedda Lettice Matthew Morrison Jim Lehrer Olympia Dukakis Louis Zorich Michael Moore Sally Kirkland James Conlon Dr. Ruth Westheimer Alan Cumming Frank Perdue Jerry Orbach

And only one gave me trouble!

Not Exactly Martin Scorsese

orange light
   red light
      green light

yellow cab cascades down the avenue

 I'm strapped behind the steering wheel

beginning a twelve-hour shift—

 mental movies begin nightly show-time

in my brain's musty Cineplex

 the nude metropolis becomes a backdrop

 creating film neurotic

I. Sights Through the Windshield

 1ˢᵗ Feature Film of the Mind

a wasn't-there-yesterday nail salon
 displays tacky signs in glassy windows
appears left of my need-of-a-wash sedan
 stuck in traffic—
seen-it-all eyes peep at Asian women
 with hair thick as lo mein noodles
scraping last week's nail polish off yuppies
 sitting under naked bulbs—

could these manicurists be descendants
of the ancient Princess Turandot
who embraced vanity—but feared love—
or are they—as rumor has it about nail salons
popping up like Starbucks all over town—
really hookers who disguise themselves
by cutting toenails off bulldozer women—
unaware that their smiling servants
hoard gold between seductive legs
after giving peppermint massages
in back rooms

stop & go

   potholes & horn-honking

stop & go   pickup & discharge

   beware Jersey drivers

collect dirty money laden with germs

   give out paper receipts

avoid hitting nasty bike messengers

   honk at double-parked cars blocking two lanes

find the next dildo-brain with raised arm

II. Driving by NBC Studios

2nd Feature Film of the Mind

back in the 1960's—eyes crazy-glued
    to *The Tonight Show*—
dreaming of escape from a sleepy town
    ten years behind the middle of nowhere

Johnny Carson on TV—Mr. New York—
    gave us bare-ass images of Gotham
through black & white television screens
    Manhattan taxis amid coruscating skyscrapers
Johnny made low-brow taxi driver jokes—
    didn't know taxis had such vaudevillian drivers
thought only Audrey Hepburn rode in cabs
    after breakfasting on Tiffany's silver pancakes—
couldn't imagine making a living
    thirty-five years later—driving a canary bomb

where is Johnny now—
    DEAD, no longer making taxi driver jokes—
lucky he's not chained to a menial job
    poisoned with nostalgia

passengers sit behind my capped head

    stone-henged women decked-out in power suits

bankers lugging real leather briefcases

    they get in   they get out   some tip   some don't

sometimes I lecture   sometimes I spit

    sometimes I lecture, curse, & spit in one breath

III. Zooming Past Tad's Steaks on West 34th Street

3rd Feature Film of the Mind

peering out an airplane window
    flying South for Christmas—
cow pastures cover the earth
    like green patchwork quilts
spotted with Dalmatian cows—

wonder if the cows are content
    or do they trespass
against sister & brother cows
    like Biblical siblings of long ago—

No—these are smart creatures
    who can read the NO TRESPASSING signs
mooing in contralto tones—
    they dine on moist grass under sparks of sun
without feelings of narcissistic entitlement—

little do these belled-Bessies know
    the butcher lurks only too soon—
one day they'll be grilled & eaten
    becoming feces
falling from the asshole of a Texan—
    a fate worse than being a taxi driver

glide & slide on oily streets

    airport jobs with heavy baggage to lift

expensive tolls for bridges & tunnels

    rainstorms with broken wipers & bad brakes

celebrities who pout without recognition

IV. Passing the Public Theater on Lafayette Street

4th Feature Film of the Mind

I'm lost like a queer Lear
    in Shakespeare's masterpiece—
a dethroned king searching
    for my illusive theatrical kingdom

frustrated by fantastical dreams of fancy
    like the raving madman
betrayed by his psychotic progeny—
    (he was really no angel either)

I see the rain tumble unmercifully
    on the old monarch's white beard—
his tears mingle with lucent drops
    from an out-of-reach heaven—

urban survival brings out
    tragic flaws in the best of us
rage yellow winds & crack dens
    cursed be bus fumes

taxi driving used to be civilized

    Checker cabs with jazz blaring on the radio

courteous passengers who think drivers are just swell

    polite address requests with a please & thank you

spacious leg & butt room   hot dogs for fifty cents

    gone with the fart

V. Central Park Drive North

5th Feature Film of the Mind

once had an older boyfriend
   named Richard the Lying Heart
he acted in a play in L.A.
   sent me an airplane ticket & I blew out—
we had passionate sex & laughs
   on LaGuuuuuuuuuna Beach
long walks strolling through Forest Lawn
   peering at movie star graves—
attended a Grace Moore Film Festival
   on Hollywood Boulevard
the feature was *One Night of Love*—
   I envied Grace's high flying coloratura—
too bad she died in a plane crash—
   my steamy affair lost power
turned out to be One Week of Love
   the kiss-ass-to-celebrities-actor
dumped me—
   said goodbye in a letter
I tearfully read—
   in the brittle autumn of Central Park

city chaos & disorder

   weaving fire trucks & ambulances

usual crap—except no place to pee

   policemen giving out quota tickets for laughs

horn honking horn honking horn honking horn honking

   vans without mufflers driven by aggressive teamsters

traffic court judges who despise drivers

haughty Upper Eastside women

drunks who barf all over the back seat

fussy drag queens saying "step on it"

pedestrians shooting the finger

as I cut them off in cross-walks

newspaper editors who hate cab drivers

holdups in dark alleys by teens shooting guns

everyone in a desperate flurry

always blaming the driver for their tardiness

Park Avenue residents asking for a quarter back

loud salesmen yelling on cell phones

dirty partition windows that rattle forever

angry lovers screaming in ultra-stereo

killing each other behind my head

New York   what kind of crazy background actors

has Central Casting sent you

VI. Intermission

Time for the First Dose of Caffeine

only 11 more hours to go
  there are no fares right now it's mighty slow
    what will I learn tonight that I don't already know—
    guess it's time to tune-in to talk radio

The Cattle Call

Dawn. Queuing outside with other livestock
for a slight chance to land a gig in Delaware,
to interpret a play by Ionesco. Prepare one

monologue no longer than three minutes. Must
show ability for classical text. (Ionesco's classical?)
Interiorly, rehearsing the storm speech from Lear,

I freeze in the swirling sleet battering Times Square.
One by one, a number is given, a time to return
for the artistic lottery, a real possibility of rescue

from the *ordinaire*. My Big Moment: late afternoon
clinging to a headshot and résumé, I smile and saunter
into a casting director's office, greeted by his bored

eyes and plump body from behind a cluttered desk—
his ugly pit bull beside him, ready to growl if I hawk
my exaggerated credentials beyond the allotted time.

Name given amid nervous jitters, I launch into
memorized Shakespeare, waving my limbs
with internal conviction. Rover loudly howls

as I nervously paraphrase the Bard's verse—
my body shaking in fear of dog bite. Mr. Indifferent
who holds the dreaded power of the hook—

obviously unimpressed by my sweet sincerity
dismisses me with a New York smugness
mixed with glee. I return from theatrical absurdity

—back into the authentic world of the absurd.

Rusted Yearnings

...where the human engine waits like a taxi
throbbing waiting...
    T. S. Eliot, The Waste Land

The end of the shift, two big-haired girls
request a pain-in-the ass address in Maspeth.
Wearing heavy mascara, the floozies
from Bloomingdales pay me in silver change,

testing my super-strained patience. My body beat,
returning the taxi with shot shocks
to a garage in Queens, I see Archie Bunker houses
through my bug-splattered windshield

as the Metropolitan Opera
blasts via the dashboard radio—
a passionate Luciano Pavarotti
partnered by the ethereal Aprile Millo

tackles the love duet
from *Un Ballo in Maschera.*
Dying sunrays warm the airwaves
intensifying the musical temperature

of this diva and divo—
their vocal pyrotechnics—electric!
O that I might live for Shakespeare alone
I mournfully moan, an exhausted silent plea

while the opera stars belt high Cs—
breaking glass with stentorian tones.
One day perhaps, elusive luck will grin
and I will prevail sensationally—

my own artistic fireworks soar,
tapping reserves of fallow talent.
Meantime, I settle for Verdi in the fast lane
as winter dusk descends on muted desires.

A Taxi Driver's Die Götterdämmerung
September 11, 2001

My downtown passenger, a banker from Barcelona—
we spoke of my love for Montserrat Caballé
that pristine day, driving this—Señor Financier
to the brass portals of American Express,

temple of commerce on Hudson's shore.
Early in the morning, I yawned tired air,
he paid the meter's fare and said *adios.*
Zooming across the Westside Highway

in my yellow zephyr—
time for tourists at the Marriott Trade Center Hotel,
renovated midget adjacent to the looming twin giants.
Respite in the hack stand, I waited for an anxious hand

to hail my trusty Chevrolet
and whisk me away to another part of the island—
hopefully, filling my poor palms with crisp bills.
Feeling a whiff of the almost autumn breeze,

my bald crown hugged the headrest,
lids lightly closed for a needed snooze.
Without warning, an earth-shattering—BOOM
sounding like a million tympanis,

magnifying into decibels of Wagnerian proportion.
At first I thought it a bomb—like the assault of '93—
leaping from the cab, heart drumming,
eyes glanced toward heaven.

Elastic flames like a snake's tongue
lanced through north tower's steel skin
as a new epoch of terror fermented in fire.
Beams ripped amid primal screams,

sparkling glass rained down on my head
like waterfalls made of crystal confetti—
fumes of sulfurous clouds sparked fear,
the world shifted, seared in a crimson blaze of hate.

Like a mortal fleeing an incinerated dragon,
I escaped into my idling car—dented by debris—
explosions cracked like operatic thunder
while frantically clutching the steering wheel

for blessed life, afraid of what might come—
numb and dumbfounded in my own Immolation Scene.
A frightened foot pushed pedal to gas,
the auto dashed like a frenzied Valkyrie

toward Midtown, amid nervous skyscrapers.
In the rearview mirror, Valhalla
of the gods of gold and power
burned behind. No lyrical Rhinemaidens

or Brünnhilde's heroic high C
soaring over symphonic orchestra—
only my sea of briny tears, *pianissimo*,
accompanied by sirens.

Claiming the Stars

For Lola Dunn

I'm a worn cabby—three-in-the-morn
   haul'n home—boozer-snoozers
      WGBO jives the radio
         jazz drives on the Brooklyn Bridge

zoo-be-doop zoo-be-doop zoo-be-doop-doop
      lah-da-doo lah-da-doo lah-da-doo-doo-doo

day scrams—moon jams
   East River flows—under the glows
      high flute toots—steel cables swing
         jazz rumbles on the Brooklyn Bridge

lah-doo-dee-dee-dee   lah-doo-dee-dee-dee do-dah
do-be-dee do-be-dee MMMMMM MMMMMM

muffler sputters—sounds saxy
   be-bopping wind—cuddles taxi
      sways yellow auto—to-the-rhythm
         jazz scats on the Brooklyn Bridge

Should I have loved you when we met
                waking tomorrow will I regret

Sarah—Billie—Ella
   filling my brain's empty tank
      honey tones soothe the soul
         jazz goddesses on the Brooklyn Bridge

You're never alone when I'm your baby
        can't love you now—someday maybe

trumpet seduces sweet melody
   time repeats—between the beats
      another era—it's the 50's
         jazz thrives on the Brooklyn Bridge

swish-boom-swish-swish   putta-pum putta-pum
      putta-pum putta-ping SHAAAABANG

cymbal sparks light the dark
   for a brief moment I possess the night

Redemption at Bluestockings

For Rita Montana

In a radical bookstore, nestled snugly
between Chinatown and the East Village,
a poetry reading proceeds on a pumpkin-scented
October night. A dozen or so Virginia Woolf-types

dressed in Soho black, sit in a collective trance
spellbound by words of a histrionic scribe
sewn in this garden of ideas—fiercely dedicated
to the daughters of Sappho. A busty bard

graces the podium with unabashed simplicity,
her face like the face of the farmer's daughter
out of *American Gothic.* Under a twist
of salty hair, a la Katherine Hepburn,

ardent eyes proclaim: I'm proud of my dykeness!
Words spin elongated, purple-hued tones,
a tease with a sexy villanelle
grabs the girls by literary breasts.

Not-so-lighthearted females moan
bobbing heads in unified approval
as their partner in rhyme pours out puns
commanding the nose-ringed crowd

like a Druid priestess. Lyrical stanzas
peppered with devilish devices
concoct a word brew—dazzling
the humble home of feminist books

cheering from eclectic shelves
and praising the senior sister in the struggle.
After pastel moments, a pin-drop silence,
hearts thump becoming an accompaniment

for an incestuous sestina—
the life of a ravaged soul sings naked,
its spirit of survival floats through the air
between long Chekhovian pauses.

Tears triggered by the fluidity
of repetitive end-words
dissolve quickly into absolved mist—
causing pink-haired women to cry.

Cleansed, the blood-washed Muse ends,
arched eyebrows remind all:
To Be Continued...
cognizant a writer's pen shall never cease

until hearing mysterious Death
recite its own book of verse:
Poems of the New Perspective—
in the tranquil peace of the next realm.

Winds of Change for an Infant Century

Spontaneity, that wild ride of cerebral glee,
a lack of it, these lacquered days of war;
wistful bluebirds glide wavering wings
from rotting eaves in killer heat

to branches of birches, without glorious song.
Grass grudgingly sprouts through sidewalk cracks,
its renegade spirit trampled and depressed,
the sea's waves lackluster, metronome breaks,

boring to bathers prepped for spectacular shows
of aquamarine splash. Somnolent employees
snooze to employer's chagrin, embryonic dreams
forgotten, appearing at lunchtime delicatessens

between bites of bologna and American cheese.
Magnificent words crippled, deformed before birth
as eddies of wind howl with rehearsed rage
at defiant clouds, refusing to evaporate

and reveal thousands of opalescent shrouds.
Long winters, short summers, non-existent
autumns and springs, time has outgrown
its churlish smile of mischief. Yet, fat sopranos

sing Ariadne's arias despite costume constraints—
poets write sonnets as the moon yawns,
syncopated children swing til doomsday
littering saffron-draped parks, old women

knit sweaters for militia guarding mosques
or circling the arid deserts of Iraq. A cell phone
world endures dial, hang-up, dial, hang-up,
a humankind rigid, unable to (spur-of-the-moment)

create whimsy in small quotidian tasks
buried beneath mind-shattering challenges—
unable to convert tyrants in fits of so-called
holy light, until death calls, and eternal dialogues

commence between regretful corpses and worms
under marble tombstones—carved by stonecutters
watching anemic clocks, anticipating their own release
into dreamlike hallucinations of cheap beer and tears.

Jersey Soothsayer in a Future Yet to Come

You must bear with me.
  Pray you now, forget and forgive.
    I am old and foolish.

        King Lear Act 4 Scene 7

I long to awake from this geriatric nightmare
back in time—to the 1970's,
even though the last decades of the Twentieth Century
were swallowed whole, stuffed & gloated

by the hoopla of the New Millennium.
It débuted like a cheesy stripper from Vegas,
floated in with lots of ostrich feathers & sight gags—
but when the goods were delivered, the only visible

prize, sagging flesh on an empty-headed chick.
Carnal lights of New Times Square illuminated
hoards of T-shirted tourists, madly swarming
to stake their claim in all-the-fuss. After boom years

passed, shellac on the streets cracked, thousands of
dumbed-down children stormed avenues, smashing
windows in search of bread & jobs, unable to read
instructions on video games in arcades—withering

like dying theme parks. Americans tire easily of old toys,
they must be drugged with pop-cultural pills
producing infant gratification. Mr. Mickey Mouse
soon became uppity & snarled at politicians

retreating back to the pale green of Florida suburbs.
One by one, hookers reclaimed sidewalks
in front of crumbling theaters—
long closed for lack of interest in *The Lion King*.

Sidewalk gamblers blossomed like poppies
entertaining soldiers protecting cash machines—
ignoring pot dealers tap dancing on Broadway
hawking the finest smoke this side of Vietnam.

Forced to leave in a great exodus of indigents,
branded poor, hauled across the border to Jersey
with bankrupted bohemians—
I long to return to the once high-horsed city

filled with bittersweet memories of my rainbow past.
New York, you graciously rolled your red carpet
to Wall Street Royalty—
eventually that rug was stained with dripping blood

of financial entrepreneurs—jumping from windows
of opulent co-ops, expensive mortgages defaulted
after real estate bubbles burst. Affordable apartments
at last, only tenants are cock roaches—neighboring

with Mafia gentry, since the homeless were bused out,
exiled to tent-camps in Newark
& the well-to-dos locked behind gated communities—
traveling exclusively in cyber space. In the creative

years of Warhol, Ginsberg, my soul was charged
by sparks of a diverse city, electrifying aspiring artists.
Greedy land developers kissed City Hall on the lips
& after generations of marriage—

divorce came in the form of eviction notices
tacked on boarded doors of low-rent denizens
whose unfair settlement, a one-way ticket—anywhere
off-island. Yes, I will reappear again,

a hairless old man strolling the boulevards a last time.
I will breathe the stale air of a town that inspired poetry
& initialed love on my heart with Art's knife.
I'll be there, when the economic pendulum swings back

& I can beg carfare from this strip mall in Paramus
where I rest my head under a cardboard house—
clutching a faded headshot, & waiting, waiting, waiting...
as a yellow wind whistles beneath a sky of starless black.

Davidson Garrett

Davidson Garrett is a native of Shreveport, Louisiana and trained for the theater at The American Academy of Dramatic Arts and at The Herbert Berghof Studio in Greenwich Village. A graduate of The City College of New York, he received a B.A. and M.S. in Education and was an elementary school teacher in the South Bronx for several years, developing arts curriculum for early childhood students. A member of SAG, AFTRA, and AEA, he has worked in theater, film, and television since 1973.

His poetry has been featured in *The New York Times*, *The Unknown Writer*, *Xavier Review* (New Orleans) *Sensations Magazine* and *The Wild Angels Poets and Writers Anthology* published by The Congregation of St. Saviour at The Cathedral of St. John the Divine. To subsidize his art, Davidson has been a New York City taxi driver for over 25 years.